## About the Author

Abu Ishahaq Hossain is a bilingual poet, researcher, writer, translator, lyricist and television program presenter. He achieved his Ph.D. on Bangladeshi saint poet Lalon Fakir. He is a die-hard cultural activist. He is the founder and president of Lalon Research and Culture Foundation. He has been researching on different areas of literature and philosophy. He has twenty-five books to his credit.

# Sense off Sense

# Abu Ishahaq Hossain

# Sense off Sense

Olympia Publishers
*London*

**www.olympiapublishers.com**
OLYMPIA PAPERBACK EDITION

A CIP catalogue record for this title is
available from the British Library.

ISBN: 978-1-80074-331-1

This is a work of fiction.
Names, characters, places and incidents originate from the writer's
imagination. Any resemblance to actual persons, living or dead, is
purely coincidental.

First Published in 2022

Olympia Publishers
Tallis House
2 Tallis Street
London
EC4Y 0AB
Printed in Great Britain

# Dedication

Morsheda Akter: The source of my inspiration

# Acknowledgements

I'm very much blessed with a lovely son, P. M. Hamza Sindid, and a beautiful daughter, Maisha Maliha Ipsita, who always inspire my spirit to be creative. I do remember the name with importance Morsheda Akter, my sweet wife, without whom nothing could have happened in my life. Besides this, I would whole-heartedly pass my gratitude to the noted scholar, Professor Quamrul Ahsan Chowdhury, who always loves me and erases all of my agonies. Special thanks should be pledged to my niece, Taslima Khatun, who always cares for me a lot. Finally, I should pledge my gratitude to Olympia Publishers for publishing this book with utmost care.

# Contents

# Open Door

I love the door…
I let all my dreams be swung on the door
So that every bit of wind in and out
Can touch and toss it.

Room never attracts me
Rather I feel suffocated
Room to me is captivity;
I want to let all my imagination be liberated.
I need door, not room:
I dream of the door — the open door
Where every bit of sunlight and wind
Can easily get in and get out.

I don't like to be captivated and made enthralled
But to unchain everything
What the open door does.

# Belief

Is
An
Ignorance
To
Unseen.

A bird doesn't bother about the unseen
A squirrel doesn't pay heed to heresy
A dog doesn't dream of future gain
A fish doesn't desire outsourcing supply
A tree doesn't content itself with false promise.

But a man does all these.

# But Still I Wanna Love

In my very early boyhood, I loved a moth
Keeping it within my palm, I hugged it, kissed it
In recompense it poisoned me
My palm, mouth were tainted.

In my adolescence I loved a butterfly
I offered my rainbow, torrential fountain
Yielded all of my dreams to it
Spent my whole pubescence chasing after it;
Thieving my dreams
It flew away cheating me.

In my youth I loved a beautiful woman
I pledged my future, my blue-heart-sky
All of my happiness, garden full of red roses
Virgin morning glow, crepuscular evening;
She splinting my heart gave me dark night.

But still, I wanna love the moth, butterfly and woman
Still, I used to love all irrespective
Coz, only love is the replica of love.

# Desert

Seven oceans in my eyes are flown on
Thirsty Sahara is in heart, I'm a lone Island
No green, no tree, no rain, chameleon,
Only simoom breaks my hope-brow, elevate-dream-land.

I dream of chirping in my evening sky
Only giant fire-ball kisses on the void
An ever-thirsty rain-bird longs for cloud
But the heartless cloud flees away.

Oasis is a far dream, hence, I want to love
Fool I am, I solace self with fallacy;
Forgot, everybody doesn't deserve love
Tear can't soothe a burnt heart or make it mushy.

I'm born to be burnt and to weep only
I shouldn't hope for zephyr, green-valley.

# Smile

Pearl in oyster, moonlight in the moon
Fragrance in flowers, ripples in river
Women of heaven, pleasure evermore
Nothing is matched against a smile.

As music to tune sweetens the audio
Of the song, breeze does to the warm weather
Likewise, smile soothes burnt heart forever
Love and life are fact, smile is video.

Frustration kills dreams, snatches life-energy
Winter causes leaves to fall from the tree
Smile is rainbow that forces black clouds from the sky
Smile brings sun ray, makes life joyful and free.

Let's paint smiles on our faces always
Don't let time be spared and miss happiness.

# Corporate World

The womb is rented; mother's milk is on sale
On auction is care of father for money
Merchandised love, hugs, humanity
By multinational companies in a large scale.

Everything is sellable commodity
Prestige, honor, emotion or feeling
With money you can purchase love, puberty
No matter you can enjoy even killing.

Creating crisis is a market policy
Starvation, trepidation, extremism
All these are back stage selling strategies
Nothing but money; rubbish is creed, belief, ism.

The blue sky, green forests; all are corporate
Stuffs; skies, forests not for all but separate.

# After life

What does happen to a shooting star in the aftermath?
Does it carry its past memories of past life?
Is Socrates now enjoying glory for his naivety?
Or Shakespeare celebrating his fame after death?
If not, in what way does Socrates enjoy his gain
Why Shelley became poet not being a businessman
Why a Prophet rejects luxury hugging self-pain
So much tombs and cenotaphs for what are built on?

If we don't get share of memories, gains and pains
If everything is lost, don't continue any more
If clouds get over just after the rain pours
If there is no end of the journey of time-train
Then what is life, after life, what is gain or loss
Why is so sacrifice to get divine bliss?

# Freedom Fighter not Terrorist

All proletariats living for the fight are terrorists
To them who snatch right, liberty are the bourgeoisie.
How the struggling people could be defined like this!
Lion hunts deer for his luxurious feast
Even so he is not criminal but
Deer fight to live is marked as rebel
In the history; law is passed to root them out,
Openly shoot them for sending to hell.

Che, Mao Zedong, Mandela or Stalin
Were terrorists? They fought for liberty and rights.
Then why the people of Palestine
Or Kashmir will be treated as terrorists?

Should storm be defined as a seditious gush?
Condemn them who destroy natural balance.

# In Quest of the Truth

Stars and Planets hover in the sky, beneath it are
Land, mountains, seas, trees, birds, animals and us
How did all these come into being, get birthed?
Does anything beget one by one having been queued?
Did anyone create all these, or they are self-created;
If there was Creator where is He now?
If there was none, then, creation got started how?
Or was He there? But now He is no more — dead.

In that case how everything is in order
Who controls cosmic, earthly rule of life?
Natural force? okay, what's happened to a newer
Situation arisen? we have to arrive
In a conclusion, if being comes from naught
Who controls everything; there is a Creator.

# Fakery

Capitalism is like poisoned honey
People swarm to it like bees— Arundhati Roy

Saints and soldiers are tools of capitalism
States and temples are the schools of cheating
Welfare and salvation are nothing but trickery
To dominate people by different isms.

Temples and states are both raised on the blood of fools
Technology and progress are civilization
What's recorded in history is a mistranslation
By the cheater to make commoners fools.

Temples beguile folk for dream of paradise
States speak of welfare and comfort — bogus
Temples and states suck blood of the indigent mass
Saints and soldiers have nice building-high-rise.

Bees sucking nectar leave stool and people get honey
Likewise, losing rights and liberty we only get money.

# Let Bygone, Be Bygone

Season to season nature changes its color
In spring gardens are lustrated with colorful flower
In ebb and tide the river changes its shape
Time to time the sky also becomes cape.

In need of time, time itself alters its motion
The stars, planets, satellites fall in confusion
Become derailed, causes cosmic hazard
Even in course of time changes the notion of God.

Likewise, human also changes to survive
Consequently, the palace replaces the cave
Alike, love, emotion, passion and compassion
All changes in genre. The same happens to prayer and
devotion.

Trees, rivers, skies, flowers, notions, thoughts all these are
Changing, why not we? Let's love; nothing is forever.

# To Be or Not to Be

To be or not to be that's the question—Shakespeare

Hypothesis, thesis, antithesis, synthesis
Surmise, confusion, faith, devotion, but
Decision comes from explanation turns naught
Even so we believe in deducing as the truth all these.

The sky has no true entity but the helium gas
We see a star-full blue sky -  the miss-notion
Civilization marches on technological invention
Unseen God is supreme, believes the mass.

What I believe you don't, conflicts demean humanity
We all just are believers, not human beings at all
Guessing could be a fact or not, or a true entity
What we see is the truth; trees, flowers and waterfalls.

The sky and God to be or not to be, but
Helium gas, human and nature are a fact.

# Man and God

God does not create man but man has created God —
Feuerbach

No history has recorded man seeing God
Question is how the idea of God comes
Is it a notion that comes from an egg-head?
Or tact for ruling fools by cunning frauds?

How did God speak to man sitting naught?
Did He come down on earth, if does, in which figure
What was His language, Hebrew, Arabic, Sanskrit?
How did He become the source of all power?

How was He revealed on earth in which medium
And not for others but only for human is religion
Why no other species did get Prophet,
Sermon, scripture: are all these men's creations?

Commonsense unknots riddles with a nod
God does not create man but man has God.

# Power and Peace

Survival of the fittest —Charles Darwin

Atom bomb, hydrogen bomb all these are
Not for existence or need but for power
Cat wants to be lion, rat a tiger
Rivalry goes on to be superior.
Killing, raping, snatching, domination
All are for so-called civilization
Everybody wants superiority, for this
Not a garden but they set up a nuclear pan.

Oppressed inflated lea cries for sun rays
The tyrant Banyan tree arrogates all focus
Storing dynamite in cotton-made house
We dream of a peaceful world for us
What a funny game really what a fuss it is
We all dream of power but speak of peace.

# Religion and Politics

Religion and politics are alike facts
Both have the same goal, it is to grasp power
Techniques are all these whether sword or prayer
For ruling the fool, they adopt different tactics.

Prophet and politician do the same for the same goal
Religion and politics are different referents for the same
Due to time variant but not phenomenal
Both are factual cunning worldly games.

If today's politicians came in the past wished to be Prophet
Prophets coming now would become politician;
As fallacy is an art of political fixture
The same are sermon, divinity, devotion and scriptures.

Religion with no political power is dead
Politics is modern replica of creed.

# Go Away the Ungrateful Bird

I opened the door of a lustrous cage
And let the bird fly away apart
I was wrong; no wild bird is to be pet
But I pledge her my virgin-white-heart-page.

I thought I could get everything by the love
I was beguiled by her cunning acting
Didn't understand all those were bluff
The bird never loved me, but was cheating.

The tide which wants to get back to its own shore
Trying to keep it as its own is just idiocy
Wanting to hug the blowing air is folly
I will love the wild in life no more.

Go away the ungrateful bird to the forest
I'll be all alone for coming days, best.

# Agony of Water

I quench your thirst but you make me vapor
O sun, what kind of love is it you give?
Enormous care for you I must have
In recompense you burn me forever.

I make a dry-river overflow but you
O river, condemn me as a heart-breaker
None to understand making me pauper
River, you get entity and shape, think of it for moments few.

You get more praise, more poetic hymn
O cloud, think of you who you are
Burning me, I gild you rainbow color
Okay, I only want you, sunshine.

My only solace is I am for all
No matter, crush me like fallen pebbles.

# Hunger and Humanism

Tiger hunts deer for its hunger; it's a need
Bird kills insects for its own survival
How could we condemn them as criminal?
They do these not for luxury but to eat.
If they don't kill, they won't live on the earth
Oppositely preys also have right to live on
Killing and living coexist in the hearth
Correspondingly march forward civilization.

People stanchly speak of humanism
Boosts of its importance with high vocal
But what's to take hunger or ism
What should be more emphasized, more focal?

Hunger or ism debate can go on
Ism fails if hunger is not abandoned.

# The Alone Sun

Burning myself, I give light to you all
In planets love and life all you get is
Offshoots of my bleeding heart—that rays;
You get pleasure moments, mine is black hole.

Planets and satellites are mine each one knows
But I'm all alone; they all orbit me
For their own self and for own existence
None concerns to me- you, they, he and she.

Everybody takes from me - give and give
Relation we have — one sided relation
At the end of day nil is my gain
I'm born for to give, poison of woe I sip.

You are all amazed seeing vast oceans
No-one knows it has so much lamentations.

# Existentialism

If I get back memory of life again after death
Or come back once again in this same fashion
Nothing destroys or dies science makes soothed
Body, mind, memory all perish away, evolution;
Molecules exist, transform, lost shape and shadow
Then where am I, where remains my existence
If I lost all these I have here in my possession
How could it be me in this universe-meadow?

Fallen leaves take away all memory with decay
Why do not new leaves carry it in their new life?
Touching the estuary when rivers meet the sea, okay
It also loses all its past mingling with sea becomes naïf
Mingling does not carry origin or keep past shape
Next life or after life all these are mere false and fake.

# Soul and Salvation

Flesh, blood, bone, nerve cell, heart, lung, vein, kidney
Body is kept on running by oxygen
Where the soul lives in body by what way
Dream, gain and pain, we get for what reason.
Theologians say body and soul are separate
Entities, temporal and undying
Soul is said to be eternal eerie
Body is made up of blood-semen excrete.

Body and soul are like lamp and fire
Reciprocal and supplementary to each other
No soul but body, *Charvaka* believes
Have and have not an unending debate goes on
If it has, then, decaying body soul goes where?
If not, how comes talk about salvation.

# No Man's Land

Heaven and hell, there in the middle is no man's land
Theist and atheist two parties are there in the world
Lure, covet, punishment only stuff they bother for
All these are give-and-take relation nothing more.

Lover and beloved satisfied with this exchange
None cares for actual love relation
For adulation God gives in rendition
Paradise, otherwise hell is His tough promise.

A sycophant crow gets its food in a golden cage
None pays heed to the cuckoo that sings sweet for love
Even a rapist and a killer is a sage
If he serves temple, God pours blessing's puff.

Atheist gets luxuries, theist comfort from God
Lover gets nothing being in no man's land.

# Let's Talk about Human and Humanity

Color, petal, fragrance which part is rose
Limbs, body, soul where lies the man
Each of these is separate part not full pan
It's not possible to be whole leaving anyone.

High and low, white and black everybody is human
Enchaining in cage if we tell bird to fly
How could the bird fly in liberation?
Likewise, differing humans by the cunning sly
In terms of religion, politics, nation
Human cannot be human as a whole
They are continuously making us fool
Tempting with a dream of civilization.

Not establishing man as true human
How could come serenity, true civilization.

# Unconcern

Night does not know the value
Of darkness
Similarly, day of sunbeam
Sonority does not of silence
And life does not that of dream.

Air does not know the value
Of music
Similarly, the river that of wave
Mountain does not of its peak
And hoard does not of cave.

Bird does not know the value
Of flight
Similarly, eye not that of tears
Firefly does not that of light
And ear does not that of sound.

Gain does not know the value
Of failure
Similarly, comedy not that of tragedy
Naught is not aware of the value of pillar
And pleasure does not of agony.

# Dependency and Love

Does the star love the planet?
If not
Why they are inter-twined?

Does the river love the sea?
If not
Why they are inter-flown?

Does an animal love fellow one?
If not
Why they have been together in hoards?

Does a human love another human?
If not
Why they initiate institutions to come close?

Does the devotee love God?
If not
Why are there so much religions and doctrines?

Answer is simple
No, no one loves coworker.

Stars and planets are inter-twined for a cosmic balance
Rivers and seas come close for manifestation
Animals live together for security
Human becomes united for increasing power

God and devotees are insane only for gain.
All those are dependent on each other.

But
I
Love
You
Not for any gain
Only for love.

# Death

What is death?

Lifelessness, destruction,
Decay, transformation
Or
Is the process of evolution?

How does lifelessness transit?
How does destroyed or decayed
Come back in form?

If it is evolution
Then
How could it be death?

Death is a mistranslated concept.

It can rather be interpreted
As a dysfunctional state
Of fact and phenomenon.

# Insensibility

Amazon forest is burning
Innocent wild animals, birds, green trees
Are dying of glowing tongue of wizard-fire
We are busy setting up more industries.

Iceberg is melting, drinkable water is running short
Water-animals are on the brink of extinction
Mother earth is suffering from asphyxia
Still, we discharge poison; still, we leave it on lurch.

The alluvial land of humanity turns barren
Millions of cherubs die of starvation
We are busy establishing more arsenals.

# The Last Kiss

It was a virgin sunset
Whole west sky decorated its lips
With red color lipstick…

Zephyr tossed the waves of rivers
Fragrance whistled to he-bee
Calm evening-light pat on the back of night
All the wandering birds came back to its nest.

You stood beside me
Getting back few steps
Again, got close to me
Hugged me with warm embrace
My trembling lips got life
Your lips painted life on mine
That was only once
When I felt the meaning of life
Now I am merely a tree.

# The Naught

Science pledges us

The star, the galaxy,
The Milky Way
And the Universe
Are supposed to be
In the naught.

Where we are!

The stars don't have firm roots
The Milky Way, the galaxy
And the Universe
All are rootless pauper.

What we have!

We are the child of naught
We are living in the naught
We will perish away in naught
There will be nothing but naught.

Then, why is this clash of civilization?

# River

Heart-breaking tears of the mountain
Drives away filth and fault
Takes all dirt what he can
Giving the sanctity and solemnity.

Cutting the heart of the land it flows before
Raising dance of waves to its bank
Takes the agony of the broken shore
Naught is gain in rendition of water tank.

Fulfilling the heart of land, it lost in estuary
The remnant of the broken shore does it carry.

# Civilized Captivity

We, a group of wretched people
Waiting in this side of the barbed wire fence
For immigration to be at own home
That side of the fence some known eyes are
Waiting to hug friends and relatives
We are here stopped and waiting for the call.

A dog couple hugs each other crossing the border
A cat is gaily running through the barbed wire
A squirrel plays running and crossing the border
A wagtail defecates on the fence.

We, the waiting people
Stare at the fence with fatigued eyes.

Building walls and stretching the barbed-wire-fence
We speak of a global village
What a prank to humanity!

# Shadow and the Shed

A shadow always chases after me
I want to shirk from it
I run, it runs
I sit, it sits
I walk, it walks
I lie down, it lies down.

When I put off my pant
It taps into my underwear
When I undress me
It stares and giggles at my every organ.

I find it in my bed, in my bathroom
On my bookshelf, on the reading table
On my spectacle, pocket, in my tea cup.
When I love and want to hug it
It vanishes away
Only an opaque shade remains left.

# Luxurious Life, Scarcity of Smile

Ample flat, refulgent drawing room
Luxurious bed, air conditioning
Decorated dressing room
Delicious dining table
TV, freezer, washing machine, BMW car
They have all for their comfort and grace.

But they have no sky, no moon, no dream
All the faces are gloomy
All the hearts are starved
They do not know how to laugh
How to love
And
How to be healthy.

# Love and Sex

Love lives in soul
is eternal, pleasure;
Sex lives in body
is temporal, enjoyment.

Without sex can be love
Blissful
Without love can be the sex
Rape.

# Fake Bigotry

Last night I dreamt a dream
But it seemed it was real.

I dreamt
Angel Gabriel came to me
Not with imaginary fashion
Very wrinkled skin, tampered ugly face
Bizarre eyes, strange look, sweltering lips
Smile like a basking withered leaf.

I was scared, trembling in fear.
He pointing his modest hand assured me
As if I shouldn't be panicked at the sight of him.

He came very close to me, I got straight
He whispered to my ear
All of your belief is bogus.

# Brothel is My Prayer House

Neither Mosque, Temple, Church nor Pagoda
It's the brothel which is my prayer house
Where nobody impedes me at the threshold
As Muslim, Hindu, Buddha or Christian
None to barricade me to offer my prayer
But
Welcome as a lover with lunatic smile.

It's neither Allah, God, Hari nor Jehovah
But a kind-hearted prostitute is my goddess
Who does not discriminate her lovers
As of white or of black skin
As an English, African or Asian
But hugs with equal love and compassion.

Neither to a stone-made idol
Nor an imaginary being
It's the harlot, my universal beloved, is my Devi
To whom
I acquiesce in my love, devotion and prayer
Whose love does not shed blood
Or make confrontation
But an amity, sweet toot,
Murmur, waft and zephyr
Stress the placid canopy for all indiscriminately.

I'm awake and in my sleep

Proffer my prayer to a darling prostitute
Sanctify myself as a pilgrim to the brothel
Only the brothel and my sweet universal whore
I love and aspire for my pleasure and salvation.
I dream of not getting the embrace of heaven
But for the warm embrace of my prostitute.

# Gag

My bedroom is inundated with refulgent moonlight
Naked moon jezebels evoke me in copulation
Insane fragrance mesmerizes the night.
I go out to the balcony
The sky came down to me
I kissed the sky
Stars got fire in envy, the lewd moon crinkled in jealousy
The coquette sky vanished away.

# Epicureanism, Renunciation, Realism

A pile of food, limitless luxury, colorful life
Only for off-sense
Renunciation, squalor, life of black and white
For innocent sense.

What should be taken
Sense or off-sense?

The epicure says life is only a chance
The sacrificer says monasticism is the best.
The realist says neither epicureanism nor renunciation
It is but humanism; live as a human.

# Religion

Is
Nothing
But
Is
Merely a fairy tale.

# Criminal

Tigers kill his fellow animals for hunger
Ants store food for survival
Man accumulates wealth, kills man, animals
All those are only for power.

# Superiority

Cows boast of their sacrifice
Lions proud of their strength
Men's conceit is for their domination.

Cows claim themselves noble
Lions aver themselves powerful
Men declare themselves superior.

A question mark whistles…

# Definition of God

Cats think of God like its own
Birds guess its god likewise
Butterflies sense it as their own passion
But men have no sense but off-sense.

# Alienation

It's a green assembly, a flowery kingdom
Dews cajole on the soft grass, tender leaf
Tossed by the naive zephyr; sunbeam kissed
On the wet lip of the park.

A tranquil drowsy park is sonorous
By a handsome gathering;
Someone is jogging, someone walking
And someone is playing.
Someone laughing, someone singing
Someone crying, someone groaning
All these make hullabaloo.

Here everybody is an individual
None to pay heed to none
None to share love and emotion to none
None to have sympathy and empathy to none
None to love none
Everybody is busy for ownself.

# Who I am

Am I You
Or
Are You me?

# I am Just a Human

I have surrendered my national identity card
Passport, religious identity
Community membership.

Please don't take me as an American
Australian, Britisher or Bangalee
And never treat me as
Hindu, Muslim, Jews or Christian
I hate all these;

I only want to be familiar just as a human.

# Referent

In the open horizon in an all open bothy
Lived alone a very old woman
Accompanied by innocent sun rays
Immaculate soft waft
Squirrel, rabbit, magpie, robin
Chirp with air concert
Green grass, deciduous leaves
Colorful virgin flowers.

A white skinned thirsty Englishman
Came to the bothy and asked for water to drink
The old lady gave the man
A glass of water from a silver jug.

After a while
A German came and appealed for wasser
The old lady did the same.

Then an Arabian came and requested for *ma'an*
The learned old lady responded in the same fashion.

At last, a Bangalee appeared with yarning and begged for *Jal*
The multilingual wise lady gave the thirsty man
the same water from same jug.

'Water' 'Wasser' 'ma'an' and 'Jal'
All those are the mere lingual referents
For the same being.

# Artist

No other beauty is as serene
As a woman's face
No other pep is as tender
As a woman's smile
No other canvas is as liberated
As a woman's body.

You will find me as an artist
When I will paint a portrait
On your body canvas.

# Marriage

Is
A
License
To
Prostitution.

# Wacky

What is the truth?
God
The sky
Or
I?

# Appeal

Just a single kiss
Then I will hug death.

# World of Wrongs

All the tanners start to paint portraits
All the barbers start to write poetry
All the thieves start to preach didacticism
All the butchers start to speak for doctrine of *Ahimsa*
All the lechers preside at the love conference
All the comrades shake couple with bourgeoisie
All the poets are busy in doing obsequiousness
All the artists penetrate mouth in dustbin
All the saints are usurers, put humanity on auction.

Only the mad and stupid
Dream of a beautiful earth.

# I Love You

I love the naught
I love the dark
I love the plight
I love the shark.

I love the stars
I love the black-hole
I love the scarce
I love the shackle.

I love the sky
I love the earth
I love the green
I love the hearth.

I love the bird
I love the tree
I love the bee
I love the sea.

I love all these
Because
I love you.

# Rendition of Love

I am tied with a pole
In a dried barren field
Under a naked tree by the very vulnerable
rope of love.
Every bit of dust ridicules me
Starvation and thirst have nestled me together.

Very next pasture full of fruits and green
Colorful flowers toss the air
Fragrance pats on my nose.

I didn't touch a flower
Didn't breathe fragrance, watch green
Having a satisfied glance to the naked void.

# Good Morning

Good morning to myself
It's a wonder, still I am alive.

# Reilly Journey

When the sun sets
It just hands the sunbeam
Over to the moon
When the flower falls down
It just leaves the bud to be sprouted
When the man departs
He leaves a dream for the new generations.

# You are Everything

Nothing is nothing
Life is something
But
You are everything.

# Desolation

Only a stupid and a genius can break man-made laws—
Kahlil Zibran

The sun is losing the sharpness of its radiation
Every deadfall awakens with twilight
Advent of morning is being lingered.

# The Truth

The sun rises in the East
And sets in the West
Tis the only absolute truth
Rest is the social truth.

# Disparity

Pile of foods ridicule at
The skeleton —died of starvation.

# Truth cannot be Enshrouded

Scented mask cannot eliminate
Bad odor of rotten face.

# Human is the Ultimate Truth

Visiting Europe, America, Asia, Africa and Australia;
Having pilgrimage to mosque, temple, church, pagoda
I saw nothing but humans only.

# Love

Love is a two-mouthed sharp blade
In every up and down it sheds blood.

# Relation

Relation
Is
An illusion
It seems real
But
Is fictive.

# Family

An intangible
tie of illusion
Continuous
fake acting
of
happiness.

# Let's Change Ourselves

In the summer, autumn, late autumn and spring
Earth changes its color
In the ebb and tide
River changes its motion
For getting sanctity in age
Snake changes its slough.

O humankind, let's change ourselves
For the betterment of the earth.

# After War

The sky is burning with
The fire of comet
The innocent poor earth suffers.

# Purdah

Sex and lure
cannot be covered
By the dress.

# Misfit

Maybe or may not
I am of the past or for the future
Certainly not for present time.

# Rapist

No record ever has been found in history
Of animal being raped by fellow animal
But it is happening everyday in our society.
What animals cannot do
Can it be done by human?

No human can be rapist
Not even animal
beware of rapists
Coz, all rapists look like humans.

# Evolution

Water is water
Because it is water
Air is air
Because it is air
But
A human is not human
Because he is from an animal.

# Dream of Communist Society

Man struggling for it over hundreds of years
Procures scholars and the army to face up
All these are for domination; man wants it never
Only a bee can be equal to all to make it up.

# Unconditional Love

Take away all of mine
Body, soul, breath, heart
In recompense
Just hug me.

Give whatever you wish
Darkness, rain, fire and tempest
I don't jib
But want to have you.

Go far away from me
Frustration, agony, scandal and slander
That's not a matter at all
I want to love you forever.

# Experience is not Truth

Truth is a fact and phenomenon
That does not change
Due to the variation
Of geography, environment and experience.

Time changes, matter changes
Ideology changes, belief changes
Man changes, nature changes
The sky changes, the river changes
The ocean changes, weather changes.

Where is the truth?
All those are mere experiences.

# You and Me

Only you and me
And the rest are fake and bogus.

# Un-ending Waiting

The sun is setting down
Under the canopy of dusk
South breeze touches
the lips of the restless red rose.

Tranquility comes down modestly
As the fatigue dew
Night spreads a dark curtain
Over the trees and grass.

All the birds are returning back nest
But I am waiting on line
I am waiting, waiting and waiting
To hug you, to love you, to kiss you

But my waiting lingers to get over.

# Uncertainty

I do not know how long
This journey will continue.

This torrent river, swift air,
Light floppy clouds in the sky-river,
Planets, moons, constellations even
The stars, the feeding-house of life
Do not know about their vague journey.

Sagging waves of green-paddy field,
Dancing ripple of the brook
Vigorous current of the river,
Roaring of the sea, shining of the stars
All run toward uncertain destinations.

Dream-lover man, revolving heavenly bodies,
The universe truly do not know
How long their journey will continue.
In fact, uncertainty is the mystery of creation.

# Awakened Moon

All the chirping is ended over
Only a faint whisper of sky grasps me
Like your credible hand.

All the flowers are sleeping
Only the tear of night
Rinses the exhausted buds
Like your nectar-caress to my dried lips.

All the brooks, rivers, valleys
Canals are dried up
Only a forlorn turbulent current flowing over
Like your memory in my lone heart.

All the stars are drowsing
With insane eyes
Only a moribund moon awakens whole night
With sleepless eyes like mine.

# The Song of Love

Coconut leaves are glistering
In the virgin moon light
Fog's fairy pours dews
On the face of the slumbered rose
Sonorous nimble-night is insane
With open concert of the crickets.

Luminous stars are ferrying
By the boat of my love
Across the river of Galaxy
Hypnotized silence stretches an illusion-carpet
Over the dew-bathed-green-grass.

The refulgent moonlight portrays
Your face on my mirror-heart
Waft dances on my window frying curtain:

The lifeless surrounding speaks out
To me like you, evokes me
Come on my love, come on my sweetheart
Let's mingle with each other;
O my darling, o my sweetheart
I aspire your warm embrace.

Concrete reality keeps you far away from me:

Break the concrete wall of wicked time

Rebuff crocked eyes of society
Be insane like me and soothe my reckless heart.

Love means a trusty kiss
Of bees on the flower.


Man lives for love, man lives in love
Man loves and combats for love
Nothing but love is eternal
It's the only cause
Why a lover can renounce the world.

# Man behind the Screen

Like still, mild generous jar water
The man is mute.
The eddy wind thrashes earth,
Trees, the fragile stream;
The calm-jar-water smiles.

The man is constant like mountains:
The snow of sorrow melts
By the glow of patience
The success flows out bursting
The corner of full heart
The man is unvarying with pent-up joy.

The juniper man pirouettes
In the clumsy bed of rage
He neglects glorious light
And shrinks like a touch-tree.

He is the man keeping into his heart
Thousand oceans of love
That burst out like the spring
And amalgamating with everything
To be very common to all.

# Devi and Devotee

This is my submission
A complete self-submission
Only to you
O my Devi I offer my heart-flower
To your worship.

No — no hope to get return
It's devotee's satisfaction to offer self
Only for your pleasure.

You may have many devotees
Many may offer themselves to you
You may be for many devotees also.

But my Devi
It is me, worship none but only you
I don't bother for your embrace
But to offer myself
Prepare myself
As your true devotee.

The sky is your abode
Everybody believes like this
Everybody offers their worship in void
But to me, you, my Devi not in the sky
I installed you in my heart-temple.

To everybody you are mere a stone-made idol
Without heart, without love;
But Devi, to me, you are incorporeal
Animated being who controls my palpitation
Every breath
Devi to me, you are oxygen to my life.

# Waiting Forever

As the bird flies away leaving the tree
As the ship goes away leaving the harbor
Like these you go away leaving me
Sprinkling the freezing snow of sorrow
On the warm land of my love.

As the roller goes over crushing all
As the flood comes breaking the heart of a brook
You crush my dream darkening flowery morrow.

As the tree waiting for the next sprout
As the Rain-bird aspires for rain drop
Like them
I will be waiting for you sitting in a melancholy-garden.

If the sun does not rise again
If no prayer house awakens again
Even then I will be waiting all alone
As the winter garden for the spring.

# Beholding God

More than fifty years I had been going to Pilgrimage
From Mecca to Bethlehem, from Kapilabastu to Kashi
In search of God's blessings, but did not get.

More than fifty years I had been visiting
Mosque, temple, Pagoda, synagogue, church
For getting embrace of God, but, yet to get.

More than fifty years I had been praying,
Worshiping, performing rituals;
Being a yogi took shelter in forests
Besmearing ashes in body, meditation, keeping fast
Diminishing selfness, dissolving self,
Surrendering self completely, giving benediction-
I yearned to get notice of God, but did not have at all.

For more than fifty years I had been calling on
Saints, monks, Peers, Dervishes, yogis, sages, scholars
For watching the beauty of God
But there's none to show the path.

Frustration pasted on my mind as the dark is
On the nocturnal bird's wing. Me like a blind
Firefly pirouetted in the unbreakable dark.
Devotion, faith lost in the endless black-hole
Only a Gnostic-bird crawls on the logic-ground.
Vainness, frustration, darkness…

Mind-bee hankers after the ambrosia of ecstasy
Putting off the veil of faith, ritual and showoff
Adoring heart-vessel with love incense
I offer my *Arati*[1] with tears to my beloved.
Barren mystic-land blossoms love-flowers:

Outside, incessant rain is pouring down
Wingless bird groans continuously
Air-flute breeds melancholy toots
The dark chamber of mine inundated, downcast
The groaning of the wingless bird laden the sky
Never-ending night pats on the afterglow of twilight.

Suddenly, the sadder chamber bursts into the innocent light
The submerged gloomy chamber turns into a golden palace
With the sober-clad. Thousand gardens smile gaily.
*Mage adariya obe muhuna mathukaranna*
*ma adaren weladaganna—*
(O my lover raise your head and come within my embrace)
—A miracle voice in Sinhali
Turned the sorrows into sprouted fresh petals.

With trembling, wondering look, I raise my head
Miracle glimpses flooding the entire sky.
She pulled my head, gripped in her breasts
The doors of seven paradises opened one by one

---

[1] The Hindu religious rite of worshiping an idol by waving lamps etc. in the evening.

Sky after sky, galaxy after galaxy have been within me
Her kiss took me on *Sadratul Muntaha*[2]
She hugged me; the entire universe is under my feet.
My whole body gets rocked with light wave.

I am amazed to be within the touch of God
Every organ is rinsed with her caress
Virgin dream unfolds the latent buds
No fear, no devotion, no gaps
Only love grasped my heart closely.

I curiously asked my God with trembling lips
A lot of prayers, pilgrims, divine practices
I yielded to you for getting your embrace
But you were far away from me.

Why?

She embracing me answered
No prayer, no devotion
But I am tamed to love.

I am not in Mosque, Church, Pagoda or Temple
I dwell in the heart of human.

No prophet, no yogi, no saint, or no scholar
I only respond to a lover.

---

[2]It's a Sufi term. According to their etymology it's the topmost throne of
God situated in the seventh sky where no being, no angels, no human
can go.

I sensed the morning glow beamed the sky
Pleasure-river overflowed with love-tide.
Flowers glister, butterfly dances on my chamber's wall
Sonority captured the heart of silence.

# What is Rain?

What is rain
Sunbeam, dust, heat, cloud
Or
Water?

# Sacrifice to God

What a funny game it is!
All that is being done
in the name of so-called religiosity;
The billy-goat is immolated to a stone-made idol
Cows, goats, camels are offered to the Ariel god
For salvation.

What a buffoonery it is!

The beasts are slaughtered
They are forcefully killed
How could it be sacrifice?

Self-surrender is sacrifice
But
What is going on in the name of sacrifice?
It is mere a festival of killing.

How a sensible god could be satisfied
By a forceful killing festival?
Sense it!

# Success

Is
Not to be in the top position
Not to get enormous luxuries
But
Is that which gives pleasure.

# Forget Me Not

Don't tell me to forget you
Nor you do me
Everything could be
But
Love cannot be replaced.

# Reminiscence

Gone days peep through my mind's window
Like the rising sun beyond the mountain.
Memory-sweet-breeze swings me
as the kid is swung on the cradle.

The cruel saw of time hews dreams constantly like a hewer
Sawed-dreams are crawling in the mud of reality
Like a blind tortoise.

Gone days play in a flute sweet toot eternally…
The sleepy late autumn was awakened
With heavy smoke of clay-hearths
Continuous murmuring of golden paddy,
Cute tune of pleasant maiden.

The sheaf of paddy paints the smile
On the dry dust of the crepuscular sky
As a legendary painter on the canvas;
Night falls down with keen sound
Of nocturnal mysterious bat's wing
Vapor wrapping mornings stepped down
With soft floppy paws of dew.

In the kitchen volatile smell
Of *Vapapitha*[3] seized the clock
Snail-time was stuck to the folk yard.

_____

[3] Rice flour made cake.

Eternity stopped here like a guest.

The dew-wet mild night was sonorous
By fable, *Jatra*[4] and fairy tale.
Grandma with sleepless vigorous eyes
Wrapping us with coarse blanket
Awakened the sullen drowsy moon
Telling the legendary myth of *Behula-Laxmindar*[5].
Nocturnal dews dropped down soundlessly
From the eyes of shocked luminous stars
Hearing the *Jaari* of *Alal* and *Dulal*[6].

The cruel rays of reality burnt
The green memory casting obscure shadow
Over the pilgrimage-mind.

Still sanguine eye of the city hawk
Kills the green alter of gone days.
The decayed corpse of memory is
Piled up like haycock
In the modern urban-concrete-yard.

Wounded dreams groan
With a cruel city arrow
Only gone days spread a delicious
Smell in my memory-cell
Like the steak in hotel.

---

[4] Bengali folk drama.
[5] Bengali folk tale.
[6] Special form of elegy of Bengali folk tale.

# Name

Name is a referent, subject to identity
By the name everyone wants to survive
Everybody wants to gain eternity.

Physique hides in phantom shadow of name
Everybody combats not for the soul or body
But for name and fame.

Even an ant is insane drinking
The wine of sweet name
Wants to leave behind something
God also does everything for none other
But to establish His name on earth.

Name gives shape to the shapeless
Gives the shapeless the solid figure
All's that false but name I profess.

# Religion and Science

Science without religion is lame and religion without science
is blind —Albert Einstein

Thousand questions buzzing in my head
Whether You are!
Everything is in due order
Stars, planets, all orbits, even a tree.

Someone claims it is due to natural force
Big Bang is the primordial source
Of all creations, a real cause.

No event ever occurs
Without any cause
But question is:
How did zero time come?
Who was the maker
Of
Stars, planets and cosmos?

It is affirmed
If there is no electron and proton
No force or energy can be created
Or cannot be happened any creation.
But
Where was electron and proton?
How did they come into contact?

Is it true there was no cause
Behind Big Bang? Someone asks.

Nothing is decayed or destroyed
Only changes in shape
Why not time consumed it
To pass out the game.

All these questions come to an end
Recognizing the aforementioned force legend.

No difference between force and God
But
It is merely a linguistic difference
Science and religion are twins
Difference is only
A thin line between.

# Adulation to Satan

We should worship Satan
Most gracious, most benevolent friend of ours
For whom we are blessed with this life
We get taste of love and power.

In tranquil heaven Adam was placed
Robot-like insensible in thought
By the trick of Satan Eve was seduced
Denied God's prohibition and broke the fort.

They were exhausted, unhappy
With their monotonous life
Paradise seemed to them a prison cell
And were bothering for their mute rife.

Beauty is beauty-less when it is monotonous
Damp day is worse than dark night sonorous.
Life is beautiful because of its variety in taste
Will and woe, gain and failure adorn it best.

Earth is precious, enjoyable
Coz, it is full of variety
Satan was the real rescuer of ours
Who taught us the meaning of life and reality.

God made us insensible robots
Satan gives life and sensibility

Satan is the father of free wisdom
Blesses us with real liberty.

The blue sky is unornamented
If there is no cloud
Humanitarian Satan became Satan for humankind
For his graceful kind to human we are here
We have been the super creation.

# Bird of Passage

A bird of passage brings a message
From far distance to me
All the nature draws the picture
To give a solid shape thee.

We are guests to take a rest
Stop in the station
When time's flute blows, whistle flows
We have to return to destination.

Morning dew carries the news
Of the end for the bud
Birds sing hailing the morning
Lotus gets born in mud.

Friends and foes come and go
Life moves onwards
Flows the current; it's no different
As time is on march.

As sleep brings dream sweet and scream
Happen in a moment
We hold our life with a death knife
Have to go without payment.

The moon shines mild and fine
When night comes

Storm, flood, cyclone, hurricane, typhoon
All are water when it gets calm.

Wave and ripple water is its cradle
Of ebb and tide
Life is nothing but means living
Only that I confide.

Flower's smell is a second spell
For all of the tree
Honey and nectar come together
Sources for the sucking bee.

Body is cloth or sheath
Soul is solid shape
It changes always a new one to his choice
An old one to a new cape.

The soul is a sun-bird and body-earth is its part
That orbits towards it
It's a case that a blackface
Where light doesn't meet.
In the same way light does sway
Occurs day and night
The soul is like a sun body is like a pan
Time to time it might
Change its axis.
He who doesn't meet is dead
The orbit, or who does miss.

Humans do die it's a lie
Only soul changes its motion
Like a river draws to end casting alluvial land
Reaching the confluence session.

Life is a bird of passage that brings messages
Generation after generation
In its path there's living the moth
Of illusive passion.

# Theatre

A refulgent stage is glistered with
The compassionate union of you and me
Every heart is rocked with love and romance.
Every eye finds the emotion of mutual faith.
Hugging, kissing, embracing, uniting
Sharing, caring…
All these turn to be fake
Just after the show.
Everybody is a separated individual
Everybody is an alienated self
Every dialogue is just a dialogue
Love, relation, emotion, cry
No, nothing is real at all
All is just acting
Actually, all actors and actresses are deserted.

# Tears cannot be Translated

You can break me and read my tears
But how can you translate it in words, dear.

# Language

Sound is symbol, a word carries meaning, language
Makes a bridge between two hearts, caused by love.

# Love is in Soul

Feeling, missing, emotion, sharing and caring
Not love; but a bridge to soul to soul mingling.

# Downhearted

It's a moonlit night, dew comes down
Petals weep for an upcoming dawn.

# Life

Eating, sleeping or having sex-pleasure
Not life; dream, gain and pain all these are.

# Inside Burning

Fire burns oil not only wick alone
Likewise, I'm burnt silently, can't be shown.

# Naught does not Mean Nothing

Night doesn't mean there is no sun, yes, there is
Likewise, the unseen doesn't prove non-existence

# Agony

Outside bleeding can be shown to all
Inside hemorrhage seen by none it's only your own.

# Core of Love

Fiction, non-fiction all these are stories
Feelings and emotion are love- ivories.

# Solitude

The sky is naught all alone; none is his
Stars, Planets, clouds, rainbow has no nexus.

# Coincide

Light which enlightens has its own dark
Dark which enshrouds light has a light spark.

# Broken Heart

I've no past or heritage, sweet memory
Only inheritance of mine is sorrow.

# Want to be a King of Heartdom

Ample sky is for flight, not to build a nest
I don't need kingdom; hide me in your chest.

# Experience

Expectation and achievement do not match
Life is nothing but just a fire box.

# Meaning of Life

To a child the world is a chamber of fancy
To a youth is love but to an old is agony.

# Vision and Illusion

Day and night are of earth, not of universe
Time has a start but no end; then why is so much converses.

# Distance doesn't Mean Separation

We may have physical distance far apart
But are connected forever heart to heart.

# Birds of Separate Nests

Sex is for few moments; love exists forever
We touch our souls belonging to each other.

# No Absolute Truth

Morning shows the day, it's not always right
Some sunny mornings end with opaque plight.

# Dream

Not the desire to have achievement
But to wish to change oneself, it is meant.

# Love and Care is the Best Power

A caged python by its chance
Can anytime swallow you up.
A hunter can trap or hunt a lion
Even the wounded lion
Does not spare the hunter.
A dictator can dominate the mass
By his absolute power
But anytime
The mass can overturn him.
Bill Gates can purchase servitude
Can build castles on the void
But not a single heart.

Nothing else
Only
Love and care
Can
Win over
Everything.

# Relation is Self-Based

I'm a dead dried tree
Without leaves
A flock of birds pass by me twitting
No bird wishes to build nest
Or to take rest on me.

I'm a scrub without a flower
A buzzing bee goes by me
Comes not humming
Not to hug or suck.

Birds need shelter
Bees need nectar
I've none of these
This is because none is for me.

No bird sits on a dead tree
Or comes to scrub no bee.

# Optimist

The shadow is getting longer
Nay, nay, it's not morning
It's afternoon
Like an evening bird
Just enjoy the moment.

# Smile Be the Rendition

Turn your broken heart
Into a lustrous gala field
As a garden does.

# Life

Life is like an aquarium
We're just beta fish.

# What We are

We're machine for capitalism
We're animal for hunger
We're human for love.

# Heavenly Feeling

Sex is the best recreation
Let's be Adam and Eve.

# Oasis

A deep valley
In between fine two legs
Raises surges to wet you
Come on O my thirsty desert.

# Flowering

Tick tock tick tock
Bustles the pendulum
The sexy bud unfolds the petals.

# Ecstatic Pleasure

Embracing of a frog and a hungry serpent
Tickles the triangle- shaped rive.

# Worship

Copulation is the best prayer.

# Orgasm

Mingling of thigh to thigh
Results into a torrent spring
Blossoms the best feeling of life.

# Life Love Sex

An old one says experience is life
A young one says love is life
A teenager says sex is life.
An old one has experience of sex
Love invites sex
Sex fulfills life.

# Last Realization

The setting sun can take with him
Nothing
But only its own beam.

# Injustice

Always only a flower becomes raped
Not the thorn.

# O Baby You are my World

My mind-bee wants to suck
The ambrosia of your rosy-lips
O baby I want nothing
But
The warm touch of your love.

Man requires household, land
Factory, chaste sky,
Colored garden, transparent stream,
Soft breeze to be soothed
Handful of money for survival;
O baby you are my world,
Sky, blue sea, cold touch of air
I need nothing
But
you to survive.

The sun ignites fire to eliminate darkness
The moon smiles on a sleepy flower-glass
O baby, I watch you
On my crystal-heart-mirror.

Day settles down and night appears
Earth becomes pregnant with dreams of clouds
Oasis furnishes and enlivens deserts
O baby your eternal love
Decorates my dream

Animates my soul
And enlivens me.

When the sun sets
The whole world rests in sleep
Even then my dream-butterfly dances
On your soul-flower.
One day everything will get lost
in the black whole
The sky will disappear, stars, the moon
Everything, everything will perish away
In the limitless darkness
Even then! O my love, even then
You will remain
Forever in my heart-Island;
Your eyes spread a blue canopy over the earth.

Rest of the world for the rest
But you
Only you
Are just only for me.

# Artist and Manufacturer

Dead poets run after popularity
Write for others.
Tree is an artist, flowers for itself
But others come to it for fragrance.

# Focus

The tree has flowers
It's a natural law
But that has to be blossomed
With beauty and fragrance
Otherwise, none sees it.

# Split Thought

What is indeed needed
Mirror
Or
Face?

# Population

A male and a female
Come together, get together
Another male or female comes out
The wretched world suffers from
The scarcity of human being.

# Everybody Loves Self Best

The moon is neither for earth
Nor for the sky
But survives for its own.

# Memory

Memory is a spiral binding book
Every page is separate
But
Is bonded to each other.

# Hard Talk

The Tree is as long
As less shadow it has.
The bush is as flowery
As less useful it is.

# First Lady

I was then reaching my adolescence
New bushy shame peeped through my
Secret mellifluous golf field
Desire to be Adam gushed out of me
A virgin rainbow smiled in my new world
The first time I experienced a volcanic eruption
You the experienced lady seduced me like Eve
I was thrilled.
My inexperienced cobra erected with its full hood
Your experienced hand came down
Hold the hood as a skilled snake-charmer
And pushed the raged cobra into your magic hole
Ah! That was my first celestial felicity
After then I became Man
Every Man has a first lady.

# What is Love

Attraction, emotion or feeling of romance?
Attraction is temporary
Emotion is momentary
Romance is rudimentary
Feeling of sex pleasure.
We mean all these as parts of love
Then why there's so much talk about love in history.

# Unspelting talk

Some talks cannot be talked
That doesn't mean I don't dream of you
Some trees don't flower
That doesn't mean it has no feeling of sprout
Some emotions cannot be shown
That doesn't mean I don't feel you
Some feelings cannot be expressed
That doesn't mean I don't love you.

# Happiness Varies

A sunny day doesn't mean a happy day for all indiscriminately.

# Satisfaction

I don't have luxuries,
A beautiful woman.
Nobody waits at my home for my return
Nobody waits to open the door
Nobody offers flowers
Nor anyone ever says 'I love you'.
I'm a man of nothing
But I'm a man of everything
I love women, flowers, and outings
I love to share myself
Finally, I love myself very much.

# Life is to Enjoy

Everything should not be taken seriously
Something should be let go
Because life is only a chance.

# Wrong Spring

When the bee was insane
You the flowers were cynic
After the fall of flowers
The spring came
What hell will happen?

# Destination

Pedestrians gather at the end
Of a multi-faced road
They all are sweated, exhausted
Torn up, wounded and deceased.

They all in their whole life
Fought for their own way
Rapacity, killing, massacres
Turn the beautiful garden into wreckage.

Not bother to slay their own brother
Not bother to loot their own parents' property
Not bother to burn the neighbor's house
Only to establish their own path strong
They didn't bother to destroy civilization.

At the end of their journey
Being in the same destination
They all fie upon themselves
For their stupidity, felicity, fake bigotry
And all the phonies and blind beliefs
At the end of their journey
They all are frustrated and repented.

# Love and Care

To an ant, to the trees
To worms, to the tigers
To the flower, to the bees
To the bird, to the men
To everybody
Life is most valuable;
Love and care fulfill the life
Let's dream of a world
Full of love and care.

# Ode to a Fallen Flower

(to my foster father Chand Ali's demise)

Self is the best example of loving
O fallen flower when you start to dispel
The blue sky whispers to the moaning air
The white fluffy cloud writes elegy
The mountain valley blows gently with your laments;
O fallen flower every flying bird tweets
In a melancholy voice —. Every drop of night-dew
Sketches the agony you burn into yourself.
The flowing spring murmurs in a faint throat
All the evening forest en-coated with sorrow
All these are but momentary.

Within a least time
All of them forget you,
Let to go off your memory
Everybody within a least moment
Replace you with the other
One day you are a forgotten case.

The morning sun, sprouting buds
The virgin river from a mountain chest
Aligned flying evening birds
The vesper, the moon, the twinkling stars
The calm night sky, blooming scrub
Even the garden whom once you

The fallen flower made mesmerized sprinkling
Scented colored buds, forget you.

Just forget you completely that once
The scrap of the creeper got a new life
Every bit of the soil beneath once
Was really overwhelmed, fascinated.

Now in this changing new era
In this a new age is completely replaced
By new generation.

No relics, no cenotaph, no eulogy
The new sky is filled with new clouds
The new river is filled with new ripples
The new garden is swung with
the wave of new flowers
A new flute toots a new melody
A new bird chirps in new voice
A new album is filled with new photos.

O fallen flower, you sacrificed
All of your fragrance, beauty
For the river, for the air
For the leaves, for the trees
For the birds, for the sky
For the cloud, for the mountain
But you! O fallen flower, now
Everywhere you are forgotten
To everybody you are a mere vagrant past.

# Happiness and Success

Does a tree think
Does a cow imagine
Does an ant dream
Does a hill hope
Or does the ocean desire?
If yes
Then why
 There is no competition amongst them
To surpass and kill others
Only for selfishness?
If not
Then question is:
Are they not happy?

# Still We Dream

All around the sable cloud gorges the sky
Though the fog engulfs the glow of the morning sun
Although the black-faced extremist roars like Hyenas
Still, we dream of a dew-cleansed
Beautiful virgin morning.

When all the lions and tigers
Killing humanity by their muscle power
Arrogate the forest;
When all the tender flowers raped by the dragon bee
Even then,
We dream of a sonorous consecrated colorful garden.

When an invisible enemy fades the hope
When the whole world is in quarantine
When all bosoms are trying to keep distance
Still, we dream of a world full of love
A world
Of closeness, caress and passion.

When society, state and nations generate hate
When scholars are busy inventing weapons to kill human
When all the leaders are concentrating on raising war
Still, we dream of a world free from war, starvation
A true world
Of amity, harmony and peace.